JEEP

1941-2000 PHOTO ARCHIVE

Peter C. Sessler

Iconografix
PO Box 446
Hudson, Wisconsin 54016 USA

Library of Congress Card Number: 99-76048

ISBN 1-58388-021-6

00 01 02 03 04 05 06 5 4 3 2 1

Printed in the United States of America

Cover and book design by Shawn Glidden

Copy editing by Dylan Frautschi

Iconografix Inc. exists to preserve history through the publication of notable photographic archives and the list of titles under the Iconografix imprint is constantly growing. Transportation enthusiasts should be on the Iconografix mailing list and are invited to write and ask for a catalog, free of charge.

Authors and editors in the field of transportation history are invited to contact the Editorial Department at Iconografix, Inc., PO Box 446, Hudson, WI 54016. We require a minimum of 120 photographs per subject. We prefer subjects narrow in focus, e.g., a specific model, railroad, or racing venue. Photographs must be of high quality, suited to large format reproduction.

ACKNOWLEDGMENTS

The author gratefully acknowledges the photography used in this Archive provided by Carl & Craig Mantegna, The Patrick R. Foster Historical Collection– pp. 24, 53, 72, 91; Jim Allen– pp. 6, 8, 10, 11, 14, 18, 25, 26, 27, 31, 32, 33, 35, 54, 55, 56, 57, 62, 63, 66, 67, 70, 76, 80, 88, 98, 112; and Daimler Chrysler Corporation– pp. 60, 113, 114, 115, 120, 121, 122, 126. All other photos are from the author's collection.

The Willys-Overland plant in 1948—showing a Panel Delivery, Station Sedan, Station Wagon, Jeep truck, and the Jeepster at the top. Missing is a CJ Jeep (see pages 18-47).

INTRODUCTION

It's been said that the most recognized trademark around the world is not the name of a popular soft drink, but rather the subject of this archive – Jeep. It seems that everyone knows what a "Jeep" is and the name is used by some to describe all types of Sport Utility Vehicles—even those that aren't manufactured by Daimler Chrysler, the current producer of Jeep vehicles.

Willys itself was bought out by Kaiser Industries in 1953—not for its car line but for the Jeeps. Kaiser Jeep, too, ended up being sold in 1970—this time to American Motors Corp., and again, in 1987, AMC itself was absorbed by Chrysler Corporation. Today, the Jeep line is produced by Daimler Chrysler, as Chrysler and Daimler merged in 1998.

Willys-Overland was one of the three companies, in addition to Ford and Bantam, that provided prototypes to the U.S. Army for a General Purpose Vehicle in 1940. However, it was Willys that ended up being the primary supplier for what became known as the Jeep. The wartime Jeeps were known as the MBs. The military used the Jeep in countless permutations during and after World War II, and in 1946, Willys introduced the first civilian version, the CJ-2A, which was built between 1946 and 1949. It was followed by the CJ-3A (1949-1953), the CJ-3B (1953-1968), the CJ-5 (1955-1983), the CJ-6 (1955-1981), the CJ-7 (1976-1986), and the CJ-8, also known as the Scrambler (1981-1986).

The CJs were replaced by the YJ, more commonly known as the Wrangler in 1987, and these were produced through 1996. These Jeeps can be identified by their rectangular headlights. In 1997, the Wrangler was updated and is now known as the TJ series. These Jeeps reverted back to the round headlights and were extensively updated and modernized.

Eager to capitalize on the success and acceptance of the wartime Jeep, Willys decided to build a passenger car that would retain the styling of the Jeep as much as possible. This was the Station Wagon and the Panel Delivery (1946-1965) built either as 4x2s or 4x4s. A truck version was built between 1947 and 1965, which featured similar styling.

The "sporty" Jeep of the late 1940s was the Jeepster, produced between 1948 and 1951. Based on the Station Wagon styling and mechanicals, this unique Jeep failed to gain the same acceptance as other Jeeps of the day, which explains its early demise.

Among the most unique Jeep products made were the FC Series (Forward Control) trucks produced between 1957 and 1964. Although they looked small, their bed size was comparable to other pickup trucks of the day and their four-wheel drive gave them an extra measure of flexibility.

In 1967, Kaiser decided to resurrect the Jeepster, at least in name. The sporty Jeepster Commando was not only available again as a convertible, but also as a Roadster, Station Wagon, and Pickup. The line lasted a little longer this time around, until 1973, when AMC decided to stop production.

Replacing the Station Wagon and Panel Delivery was the Wagoneer of 1963. Like other Jeeps, it too had a long production run with its final year in 1991. Based on the Wagoneer mechanicals and styling was the Gladiator pickup, also introduced in 1963. It would be renamed as the J-Series in 1971 and would stay in production, relatively unchanged through 1987.

A Wagoneer spin-off, the Cherokee, was introduced in 1974 as a sportier and less expensive Wagoneer-type vehicle. In 1977, a four-door version was added as well. The big Cherokee was finally retired in 1983, to be replaced by a downsized Cherokee. The downsized Cherokee continues to this day, after having received a mild restyling in 1997.

For a short time, 1986-1992, the Comanche pickup was available. The Comanche was based on Cherokee bodywork and mechanicals, but its days were numbered, as Chrysler preferred to promote its own Dakota pickup instead, when it took Jeep over.

The latest (and most profitable) Jeep to date is the Grand Cherokee, introduced in 1993. Chrysler felt that the market would be receptive to a truly modern and upscale Jeep and of course, they were right. Today, the Grand Cherokee is produced in greater numbers than either the Cherokee or Wrangler.

The three Jeep models currently produced will continue on into the next millennium; and we'll probably see some interesting new Jeeps in the years to come, as well.

Table of Contents

MILITARY JEEPS

This is the first Jeep ever produced—the Bantam Pilot model.

The Willys prototype was the Quad. Only two were made, and none have survived.

Ford's prototype was the Pygmy. The Ford GP, shown here, bears a close resemblance to the Pygmy and is one of 50 built with four-wheel steering.

After the Bantam Pilot came the Bantam BRC-60, of which 69 were built. Only one has survived.

Willys, Ford and Bantam were contracted to build an additional 1,500 units after the initial prototypes. The Willys version shown here, the MA, was the one the Army used to standardize over all other designs. The standardized versions were known as the MB.

Wartime Jeeps were built in some unusual configurations. This is a Ford-built GPA.

The evolution of the military Jeep is shown here. The Quad is on the left, followed by the MB, the M-38, and the M-38A1. The M-38's civilian equivalent was the CJ-3A, and the M-38A1 became the basis for the CJ-5.

1949 Willys-Overland Engineering Pack Jeep Trailer.

1952 M-38A1. The resemblance of the civilian CJ-5 (see page 28) is obvious.

M-38A1 with recoilless rifle. This shows just one variation of what the army did with Jeeps in terms of armament. The author saw one of these in 1987 during a visit to Greece, and it was still in service in the Greek Army!

1951 CJ-4MA-01 Ambulance. The CJ-4MA was a close relative to the CJ-4, which was never produced. Whereas the CJ-3s had flat fenders, the CJ-4 shows the transition to the rounded fenders of the subsequent M-38A1 (see page 14) and the CJ-5s (see page 28).

Early 1970s M-151A2 with TOW missile launcher.

THE CJ & WRANGLER 1944-2000

1944 CJ-2 AgriJeep. Although it is speculated that a few CJ-1s were built, the first known civilian Jeep was the CJ-2. The AgriJeeps were built in three series and the first of the series (shown) used brass "Jeep" emblems on the hood, windshield frame, and rear panel.

1946 CJ-2A. The CJ-2A production began in July 1945 and ended in 1949 with a total of 214,760 produced.

1946 CJ-2A Fire Jeep. A few early Jeeps were converted to fire trucks — a practice that continued on with the CJ-3Bs.

Early CJ-3B with Workman hardtop. The side curtains and convertible top limited the Jeep's appeal in colder climates, and many outside suppliers developed hardtops for it.

1953 CJ-3A set up for train track duty — definitely an unusual Jeep application.

A Pepsi Jeep, similar to the Surrey Gala DJ-3A, was used in Pepsi-Cola promotional events. The one shown here is yellow, but others were also built in blue and pink.

1960 Surrey Gala. The Surrey Gala was a special Dispatcher DJ-3A model (two-wheel drive) painted pink with pink and white striped seats and top. They were used mostly in resorts and were built between 1958-1964.

DJ-3A with fastback soft-top. The top was designed to give the Jeep a sportier look, but because it was two-wheel drive, it had limited success.

This is an experimental CJ-3B mail conversion with Koenig body. Post Office Jeeps were quite a common sight at one time. Note right-hand drive.

1962 CJ-3B. The CJ-3B saw little visual change in its long production run from 1953-1968. A 12-volt electrical system was adopted in 1957. Most of the U.S. auto industry adopted the 12-volt electrical system during the late 1950s.

Edgar Kaiser (far right) and other executives with a 1955 CJ-5. They sure look happy. Production on the CJ-5 ended after the 1971 model year.

Early CJ-5 with soft-top.

1956 CJ-5 with Jeep-a-Trench attachment and plow. Jeep tried to promote the Jeep for use in as many different applications as possible, but some of these adaptations were not very successful.

1964 CJ-5A Tuxedo Park Mark IV. The Tuxedo Park was a more "luxurious" Jeep, if one could call it that. It was a tad more comfortable than the regular Jeeps and used chrome bumpers, hood hinges, and other trim.

1969 CJ-5 with the optional V-6, which had become available in 1966. The extra power sure made the CJ more attractive.

1969 CJ-6. The CJ-6 was also introduced in 1955, along with the CJ-5. It was very similar to the CJ-5, but had a 20-inch longer wheelbase.

1970 CJ-5 with the rare Kayline Luxair Soft-top.

1970 Renegade I. With the Renegade, Jeep committed itself to producing a much sportier Jeep. Such things as stripes, bigger wheels and tires, and bold graphics would characterize the Renegade.

1972 CJ-5. This is a typical, "regular" CJ-5 without the visual punch of the Renegade. Still looks good, though.

1973 Renegade. The Renegade became a regular production option in 1974 and included the 304 AMC V-8.

1974 CJ-5.

1977 CJ-7 Renegade. This is typical of what a Renegade looked like as produced in the late 1970s. The 304 V-8 became an option in 1976, instead of being standard equipment.

1979 CJ-7 Golden Eagle. The Golden Eagle was produced between 1977-1980 on both the CJ-5 and CJ-7 platforms. It came with upgraded trim and features, but most noticeable was the large eagle hood decal.

1982 CJ-7 Limited. The Limited was a luxury package for the CJ-7 and was built only in 1982 and 1983.

1982 Scrambler. Also known as the CJ-8, the Scrambler was a pickup version of the CJ-7 and was produced between 1981-1985.

1984 CJ-7 Laredo. The name Laredo became synonymous with luxury—and not only on the CJ. On the CJs, the Laredo package, which used lots of chrome, was available during 1980-1986 on the CJ-5, CJ-7 and CJ-8.

1985 CJ-7 Laredo.

1987 Wrangler. The Wrangler was essentially a refined CJ. The rectangular headlights easily set it off from previous Jeeps.

1997 Wrangler Sahara. The Wrangler was again updated in 19907— and this time in a major way. The Wrangler featured a modern coil spring suspension and a new interior—yet, the return to the round headlights harkened to its past. The Sahara was the top-of-the-line model.

2000 Wrangler Sport.

JEEPSTER 1948-1951

1948 Jeepster. The Jeepster was the "sporty" Jeep of the late 1940s. The styling and mechanicals followed those of the Station Wagon/Panel Delivery (see pages 59-65). All Jeepsters were two-wheel drive.

1950 Jeepster. The 1950 Jeepster was redesigned slightly, using the new five-bar grille that appeared on the Station Wagon, Panel Delivery, and truck. It used chrome bars on the Jeepster.

1950 Jeepster. A few 1949-1950 models were available with the Lightning six-cylinder engine. Jeepsters so equipped have the number "6" on the front part of the hood.

1950 Jeepster. Besides the lack of horsepower, it was the lack of side windows that made them unpopular.

1951 Jeepster. The end of the line for the Jeepster was in 1951. The Jeepster name, however, would once again be used in 1967 on the Jeepster Commando.

JEEPSTER COMMANDO 1967-1973

1967 Jeepster Commando convertible. The Jeepster Commando was designed to resemble the CJs from the front but offer more in the way of passenger utility. The convertible was the top-of-the-line model.

1968 Jeepster Commando convertible.

1969 Jeepster Commando Station Wagon. The Station Wagon proved to be the most popular variant of the Jeepster Commando line, with its metal hardtop.

1969 Jeepster Commando Roadster. The Roadster was the bottom-of-the-line Jeepster; an optional soft-top was available.

1970 Hurst Jeepster Commando. Hurst, whose claim to fame was as a manufacturer of shifters (and certain truly special modified cars) teamed up with AMC to build the Hurst Jeepster. Only about 100 were built, which featured (yes, a Hurst shifter) bigger wheels, tires, and special trim.

1972 Commando. After AMC took over Jeep, they dropped the "Jeepster" from the name and gave the car a new front end. Although it isn't considered to be as attractive as the Jeepster Commando, it did have the AMC 304 cubic-inch V-8 as an option.

JEEP SEDAN DELIVERY/STATION WAGON 1947-1965

Panel Delivery prototype. Eager to capitalize on the success of the wartime Jeeps, Willys introduced the Panel Delivery in 1946 and the Station Wagon in 1947.

1946 Station Wagon. The Station Wagon, besides being roomy, was also the first American Station Wagon to have an all-steel body.

1948 Panel Delivery shared the same flat grille as the Station Wagon (see page 62) and Jeep truck (see page 66).

1949 4x4 Station Wagon (center) and 4x2 (left & right). 1949 was the first year of production of the 4x4 version of the wagon.

1952 Station Wagon. In 1950, the Station Wagon and Panel Delivery got rounded fenders and this type of grille, which used five horizontal bars.

1953 Station Wagon. This was the last year for the five-bar grille; beginning in 1954, the grille would use three bars. The only deviation would be in 1956, when only two bars were used.

1960 Station Wagon. Besides the side moldings, two-tone paint treatment, and one-piece windshield, there was little difference between it and those made ten years earlier.

JEEP TRUCK 1947-1965

1947 Jeep truck. Both two-wheel and four-wheel drive trucks were introduced in 1947. The two-wheel drive truck was discontinued after 1951. Shown is a four-wheel drive version.

1950 Jeep truck. The 1950 Jeep truck used the same pointy front grille and five horizontal bars as the Station Wagon (see page 63) and Panel Delivery models.

1955 Jeep truck. This 1955 shows the redesigned grille of 1954, with its three horizontal bars.

Jeep truck with a special body. Jeep trucks were built in many variations, such as the one shown here.

1957 FC-150. The Forward Control trucks were unusual, to say the least. They look small, but their pickup bed size was comparable to those found on other trucks of the day.

1957 FC-150. The FC-150 was based on the CJ-5 Jeep and used the same engine and drivetrain.

1957 FC-170. The FC-170 had a longer wheelbase compared to the FC-150 (103.5 vs. 81 inches), and also used a six-cylinder engine.

1958 FC-170. The Forward Control trucks were built in many variations. This one has a sliding dolly bed.

1959 FC-170 dual wheel Dumpomatic Stake. This is another FC-170 variation. Note roof lights.

FC-170 Camper conversion.

FC-170 conversion. The FC trucks were ahead of their time, as was this interesting passenger conversion built in Sweden in the early 1960s.

1963 FC-150. This particular FC-150 pickup is still in use today.

1964 FC-170 Fire Jeep. Another FC-170 conversion was the Fire Jeep. FC truck production ended with the 1964 model year—they just didn't catch on.

1963-1987 JEEP GLADIATOR/J-SERIES

1963 Gladiator prototype. The Gladiator trucks, introduced in 1963, were a truly modern design at the time and were offered in two and four-wheel drive models.

1963 Gladiator prototype. The Gladiator was based on the new for 1963 Wagoneer utility vehicle (see page 88). It used the same drivetrain and chassis as well as styling.

1963 Gladiator. The Gladiator was available in many configurations. Besides being available with three bed types from the factory, there was also a chassis cab for custom body applications.

1972 J-4000. The Gladiator became the J Series in 1972. A new grille design – the same one used on the Wagoneer since 1965 (see page 89) – became standard on the trucks as well, beginning in 1970.

1977 J-10 Honcho. Introduced in 1976, the Honcho package was mostly a trim package that gave the truck a sporty flavor.

1977 J-10 Golden Eagle. Another trim package used on the J-series trucks was the Golden Eagle—similar in concept to the CJ Golden Eagle (see page 40).

1979 J-10 Honcho. The Honcho package certainly improved the image of the Jeep truck line in the late 1970s.

1981 J-10 Honcho. The stripe scheme on the Honcho changed every year. This is a rarely seen Thriftside. Note new roof treatment that deleted the overhanging cowl.

1987 J-10. Still looking good, the J-Series were no longer able to compete effectively in the market place. Chrysler, which took Jeep over in 1987, dropped the line in the same year.

1963 Sedan Delivery. The Wagoneer was quite unusual in 1963. Besides being offered in two and four-door versions, a special Sedan Delivery was available.

1965 Wagoneer. The Wagoneer's familiar profile and look would be produced for almost thirty years!

1966 Super Wagoneer. The Super Wagoneer was the first luxury, upscale 4x4.

1970 Jeep Wagoneer. The emphasis was definitely on luxury and creature comforts on the Wagoneer. The electric sunroof was new on the 1970 model.

1972 Wagoneer.

1975 Wagoneer. The Wagoneer showed few changes by 1975. The new grille was the most obvious change.

1977 Wagoneer. Proving that the original design had a simplicity of function that sold well, the Wagoneer showed few changes in 1977.

1980 Wagoneer Limited. The top-of-the-line Limited model had all the usual luxury options as well as four-wheel drive. This would be the trademark look of the Wagoneer and Grand Wagoneer through the early 1990s.

1984 Grand Wagoneer.

1988 Grand Wagoneer. As the model years passed in the 1980s, it became very difficult to distinguish between one year from another on the Grand Wagoneer.

1991 Final Edition Grand Wagoneer. In 1991, the Grand Wagoneer was thought of as a dinosaur; a huge, passé relic from another era—yet a few years later, Ford and other manufactures are building big SUV's once again.

JEEP CHEROKEE 1974-1983

1974 Cherokee. 1974 saw the introduction of the Cherokee—basically, a less expensive, somewhat sportier-looking Wagoneer.

1975 Cherokee.

100

1976 Cherokee. There was little to distinguish the 1976 model from the 1974 models (see page 99).

1977 Cherokee Chief. The Cherokee Chief, introduced in 1976, gave the Cherokee a truly tough-guy look. The Chief was fitted with wider axles, 15x8-inch wheels, and unique trim.

1979 Cherokee Chief. The grille on the Cherokee was changed in 1979, using rectangular headlights. The Chief model remained basically unchanged.

1979 Cherokee.

1980 Cherokee "S." The Cherokee S model was a "value" leader, offering reasonable appointments at a lower price than a Wagoneer. The S was available in two and four-door versions, until it was dropped after 1980.

1981 Cherokee Chief.

1982 Cherokee Laredo. This was the most luxurious Cherokee model.

JEEP CHEROKEE 1984-2000

1984 Cherokee. The redesigned Cherokee of 1984 defined the term "Sport Utility" as it is known today.

1985 Wagoneer Limited. The top-of-the-line Cherokee of 1985 was called the Wagoneer Limited, and was basically a downsized Grand Wagoneer. It used a quad headlight treatment.

1987 Cherokee Chief and Laredo. This photo shows the sport Cherokee Chief (foreground) and the luxurious Laredo (background). The Chief model was available only as a two-door.

1988 Cherokee Pioneer. The "entry-level" Cherokee in 1988 was the Pioneer model.

1994 Cherokee Country. The top-of-the-line Cherokee model in 1994 was the Country.

1996 Cherokee Sport. The Cherokee Sport offered a good level of equipment at a reasonable price.

1997 Cherokee Country. The Cherokee was freshened up for 1997, with slightly restyled front and rear end treatments to go along with a new dash.

2000 Cherokee Classic.

JEEP COMANCHE 1984-1992

1986 Comanche. The Comanche pickup was obviously based on the Cherokee. It was available in two wheelbase lengths. It was the first true mid-size pickup, beating out the Dodge Dakota by a year.

1986 Comanche Chief. The Chief was the sporty Comanche.

1989 Comanche SporTruck. The SporTruck replaced the Chief and Laredo Comanche models in 1989.

JEEP GRAND CHEROKEE

The top-of-the-line Grand Cherokee for 1995 was the Limited. This V-8 powered version featured complementing gold exterior trim and leather interior.

1997 Grand Cherokee Orvis Edition. The Grand Cherokee was introduced in 1993 with a high level of standard luxury and comfort features. The top-of-the-line version in 1997 was the Orvis Edition. The 1993 through 1998 models share the same mechanicals and body panels.

1998 Grand Cherokee 5.9 Limited. The last of the 1993-1998 models was the 5.9 Limited, which featured the 5.9l Chrysler V-8.

1999 Grand Cherokee. The 1999 Grand Cherokee was subtly restyled in 1999 and also received a new optional overhead cam 4.7l V-8.

1999 Grand Cherokee assembly line. The Grand Cherokee is built at Daimler Chrysler's state-of-the-art facility at Jefferson Ave., Detroit, MI.

1999 Grand Cherokee assembly line. These are partially completed body-shells on their way to the paint department.

1999 Grand Cherokee assembly line. A few more operations, and these Grand Cherokees will be ready for delivery.

2000 Grand Cherokee Limited.